A Thought in mind

Scott Davies

ISBN: 9798818144092

DEDICATION

Although the material in this book has been written by myself, I would like to attribute the thought's and thinking to all that have taken the time to stop and think about this world in great depth.
Those long past
those not so long past
and those in the now

CONTENTS

PROLOGUE

"A man who lies to himself, and believes his own lies become unable to recognise truth, either in himself or in anyone else, and he ends up losing respect for himself and for others. When he has no respect for anyone, he can no longer love, and, in order to divert himself, having no love in him, he yields to his impulses, indulges in the lowest forms of pleasure, and behaves in the end like an animal. And it all comes from lying – lying to others and to yourself."

~ Fyodor Dostoevsky

DO YOU BELIVE

Can you believe
in anything at all
Is there more
Do we know it all

Some tell us how
and what we should think

But it's for us to discern
our inward thoughts

To be good and kind
is better than to be wise
endeavour to be both
is the way I'd advise

A child is taught
in the simplest form
So, he can be safe
kept in the warm

With guidance and love
begins to understand

Matures from boy
into a man

We are taught 'be good'
from young

Many forget
the good is undone

New things are fine
enrich our new world

Knowledge of truth
is needed as well

Lessons today
have been learnt in the past

But is all
that's learned
truly grasped

If we take to our hearts
all lessons taught
You have a head start
In life of a sort

Not always to riches,
fame, or success

But too

peace in your life

love

and less stress

WHY FORGIVE

Why should I forgive
those who do me wrong

They've broken my heart
hurt me so long

Eagerly waiting
and happy to see

Only the worst parts
I show
of me

How can I win
over
all those who sin

make me feel sad
so, they feel less bad

about the world
they've created

contrived over time
twisted thoughts
manufactured
in mind

It's thoughts in their head
the problems are there

failing to see
A difference between

the seen in their mind
and true reality

Now are they so bad
Are we the same

How do we overcome
the heartache and pain

Show compassion to all
never give in

The hate in your heart
that's where you sin

No one can change
what's happened long past
how lives
are moulded
shaped in a form
by those who
raised us
from infancy born

We don't realise
but deep in our soul

Everything that touched us
stays for all time

Although we don't know

It controls what we do

The way we act

It controls that too

It controls how we think
and perceive the whole world

It controls how we love

Keep that in mind

To change for the better
is hard to decide
even if we know
all we are inside

Meditate each day
to know all you are

Meditate each day
in order to see

The person you were
are in the now

Regarding the future
would rather be

All our effort
we will need
To let us become
the self to which
we strive
Too become

The self
for which we long

See the whole picture

Shape what's to come

It's only you
who can know
your true path

It's only you
who can choose
where you go

Empathy and love
will always prove right

The cruelness of life
is far
out of sight

To those
not realising
the truth in their heart

All in this world
need love and reproof

They love to give pain
can't face life alone
bring people down
needing the crown
of looking so fine
up in this world
higher than you
above all the crowd

But deep in their soul
they know very well
they are living a lie
not doing so well

too proud to admit
to the crowd
lorded from a high
They
are the one
they really despise

and what they crave
Is to love
and be loved
not be judged
as they've always judged

Unconditionally give love
to all that you meet

those in our home
those on the street

those who reject
those who resist

Freely give love
we must endeavour
to persist

It will benefit the good
may change the bad

Realise this

To give of your all
and do your best
Will bring meaning to life
This I suggest

One who
gives freely
genuine of heart
Gains love and forgiveness
for mistakes on his part

Good intention though
isn't enough

Do all sincerely
not aimed at a gain
Peace you can have
you've overcome the pain

You win at life
If you
surely try
to gain
Enlightenment

This can't be denied

TRUTH

We all tell the truth
Well, that's what we think

We never tell lies
to that we'd not sink

but the reality of truth
spoken by man
is bent and distorted
in each person's mind

The heart is treacherous
As we've been told

It clouds and diffuses
The thoughts from our mind

When lies are formed
they begin with a thought
of how you can manipulate
one's future of sort

We want to be comfortable
take easy path
Be praised by our peers
in this wish to bath

To artifice

Create the not true

Will follow you about
always with you
When
keeping false spoken

from being discovered

Leads to a stress
truth ever closer uncovered

It will consume your whole life
and ever be present
Living a lie
make being unpleasant

Speaking every truth
Is this the way

I say what I want
and don't care what I say

If it's a truth
must it be said

or should
some
of OUR thoughts
Stay kept in our head

Is it truth that you know
Or
Just a point of view
Felt in your heart
needed to peruse

Is it true you
Are right

Be on guard

Keep tabs on belief
your heart
may take over
distorting
and seeing
the world
from one's favour

An idée-fixe formed
Is not easy undone

Informed truth
only tell

Educated truth
as well

There are truths
you can't tell
some may say Don't tell a lie
May be easier to do

A truth spoken
can lead to
good intentions
being broken

A foundation of truth
will serve you
in life

Used for right reasons
stop heartache
and strive

THE PROBLEM WITH TRUTH

Truth is constructed
by all who think
they know what they see
and say what they think

But what they think
is learnt, observed

then made in the mind
to right or to wrong
taught as correct
to all who agree

But does that make it truth

or could it be
only the truth
you want to see

For truth in the past
may not be for now

understanding
can change
over duration of time

Things that we've touched
are only perceived
in the mind at this moment

A chair or a table
are not for all time

for once they were dust
and to that they will return

and that so means
truth is ever so fleeting

Dust isn't table
and dirt not a chair

but only perceived so
in a
fraction
Of time

To make something constant
takes more to conceive

and interacts with life
on every degree

To make something be
we imagine what it is

Said object
is then
only for that moment
the thing
we want
and believe
truth to be

It's not what it is
but is only in form

seen in the now
decided by mind

before
quite different
and after is too
and for other creatures
Its some different too

For everything is connected
not just by form

It's connected by thought
which isn't a thing
only the interpretation
of what we want to see

You can only tell truth
how understood in this world

Saying truth
Courses responsibly

For although it's right
to speak what is true

You know what can hurt
will you say that too

Use what you think
only for good
as truth will destroy
when told in spite

It may be true
but does this make it right

Understand
use the truth
In you

why you say what you do

don't forget

Knowing what's true
Can change
Over time
As does mankind
You and your mind

HONESTLY

I honestly don't know
Why you can't see
My point of view
comprehend
Why
I do as I do

You don't understand
You don't really know
Can't comprehend
the place that I go

Is it your fault
Or is it just me
Who can't
think like you

I don't understand
All that you do

can it be you
who can't see what I see
from your point of view
the same
As I see

IS THIS ME

Truth

You know the truth
arrived in your thought
is that the same truth to
those you've taught

Or do you think…

These all around
can't really see
they've got no idea
what I contrive to be
they must observe
what I want
them to see

Questions are wrong
not what I need
you don't know who
I am
I must teach
so, you will see
the truth from my world
how I've dictated
it to be

I don't understand
how you could think

that I lie
For I've covered my way
with all that I say …
ever so well all under veil

But people find out
for they can read faces,
actions with hands
they can sense fakeness

Soon I've climbed
So high
above all others

They're below me down
down on the ground

But ever so quickly
I forgot who I am
and think that my lies
are the truth that I am
confused at my brain,
struggling the strain
of lies I speak
inside, outside,

Can't see
or
Don't want to admit
the truth of myself
to all that I meet

Worse than that
I can't even tell
that although
I lie to them
lie to me as well

Shocked surprised
for some people see
my struggle with life

the struggle in me

I lie to myself
and to all in my world

I'm the center of which
is made in my head
and conclude to myself
everyone is
thick in the head

BRIEF THOUGHTS

Is believing seeing
or seeing believing

only believing
in what you can see

Takes out
the potential
you know
in future could be

.

If you will only go
with what you know

You'll only see that
which you know

Do you believe
in only what you know

Or do you believe
in where you could go

.

Some go to church

to see and be seen
Some go there
to say they have been
Some go there
to snooze and nod
few go there
to worship God

.

Many have a faith
Or so they say

But I wonder who
in heart and home
truly pray

Some don't believe
they form an opinion

But when death is close
or terrible things happen

God may be called upon
for help or for blame

Deep in the heart
We are the same

.

Wisdom is gained
won in a way

by listening to those
who think what they say

By those who
thought deeper

Deeper than you

Have pondered the world
and all that we do

.

Who knows best

Do you know more

Has the knowledge
to control
all that is said
Become all important
to thought in our head

does it make those
that
control what we hear
the ones to listen too
respect and reverie

.

Expert in one thing
Maybe possible to learn

To know about everything
one can never claim to discern

Could an artist
know all theories of science

Or a history professor
teach about math

A carpenter is educated
good with his hands

But would you let him
teach your children
subjects more grand?

Having a degree
in philosophy

Doesn't allow you
to tell me
how to be

.

KNOWING GOOD

Is it needed

For what

For why

How much knowledge
should you learn

acquire

Should I stop learning

My brain is not full

But the questions answered
make my peers seem small

So new I seek
Near everyday

I'm looking for something
to show me the way

But the way to what

The way to where

What does it mean

Oh, I despair

For I know what I need
to get on in this life

But
There's always a 'but'

I hunger for more

Knowing something
I don't think
can be turned

Once truth understood
there's never return

Maybe I should stop

apply what I've learned

This would be better
for me and to my concern

Ascending ascending
my thoughts go so high

But my body is week
I want to stop, 'die'
I want to attain
to the highest of peaks

not left down

down on the street

lower than this
down to abyss

A thought…in my mind
A thought I've crossed

Being so low
can give a prospective

A course
Where you can go

From the
very most bottom

You can see all

All the potential
laid before you

All the potential
One day
You could be

A LOVE SEEN TRUE

When you love true
what's to do
when the world around
attempt to destroy you

.

Why do we love

Now i see
shown by she
how I should act
How i could be

But she is
not showing

or telling how

Just being her
how
she is now

And because
i have opened

have let myself out

Exposed inner parts

Allowed them
prized out

Before i was closed

Shut tight in myself

Not aware

My shadow
Imprisoned

Shut in the dark

But if I open
the door

with the help
of a love

A little sneaks out
a bit of real self

Letting I
become vulnerable
To outside force

Feeling the terror
of the inevitable course

Surly
to come calling
at an undermined
time

But let it
you must

With wide
open arms

if you never
climb a tree

do you avert harm

you must embrace all
if you're to
love

And you must
if you wish
to receive
A return

For although
you let out
who you truly are

Love rushes in

More enters
Than can
Escape

From your
hold

Frees

Loneliness Vacates

I

How am I

All that is done
is done for the I

But in this being
you must ask why

What do I mean
what am I an

What do I do

I do what I can

But 'can' for who
'I' or' you'

I am somebody too

so
shall I work hard
for me
or
work hard for you

It's difficult to see

if I am doing for you

Is doing for you
for me too?

EPILOGUE

In a dream special things happen.
We are all in our own dream, unique to the universe but all the
same. We have the ability to stop and think, make this world better for all.
But most don't. They are busy with their own inward thoughts,
troubles.
Sometimes this is necessary, as we need to survive, but in most part
the west has risen above that despairing time, of always in need.
We have gained the ability to feed and shelter ourselves, though some
may struggle, it's mostly because of their own self-destructive mind, which
is what I'm trying to address.

The world is beautiful, and life can be full, if we were to learn the lessons
taught over millennia. Since the beginning we have been given a gift to learn
from those who went before. It's a slow work we don't realise what we are
really being shown.
Take the responsibility of yourself, to impart all your knowledge to those
that come after you in the hope they will realise sooner than you how to
make things better for them, and in doing so widening the betterment to all
around. If we all done this the world, we live in will only get better.
"Jesus said unto him, Thou shalt love the Lord thy God with all thy
heart, and with all thy soul, and with all thy mind.

38 This is the first and great commandment.

39 And the second is like unto it, Thou shalt love thy neighbour
as thyself.

40 On these two commandments hang all the law and the prophets."

Whether or not you believe in God it's worth pondering on this point a
great deal...
Why put something higher than anything you're able to attain…
Higher than perfection,

While thinking on the above DO IT!

It's for our own good.